Focus Bot: The Cure for a Distracted World

Easily Win Back Your Focus with ChatGPT

by Sugar Gay Isber McMillan

This edition was created and published in the United States of America.

All images and design elements were created by hand or sourced from verified public domain archives.

No AI-generated imagery or text has been used in this book.

Published by **The WOW Book Co.™**
www.TheWOWBookCo.com

Tiny Prompts for Clarity, Calm and Control with ChatGPT

ISBN: 978-1-967973-65-1

FOCUS BOT

THE CURE FOR A DISTRACTED WORLD

Easily Win Back Your Focus with ChatGPT

Sugar Gay Isber McMillan

Contents

WHERE YOUR HOURS REALLY GO

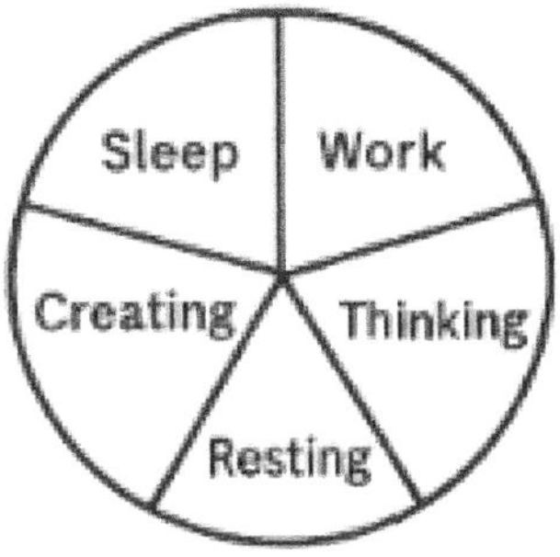

Focus Bot, help me rebalance this pie. What's taking more than it should?

DISTRACTION LOOP

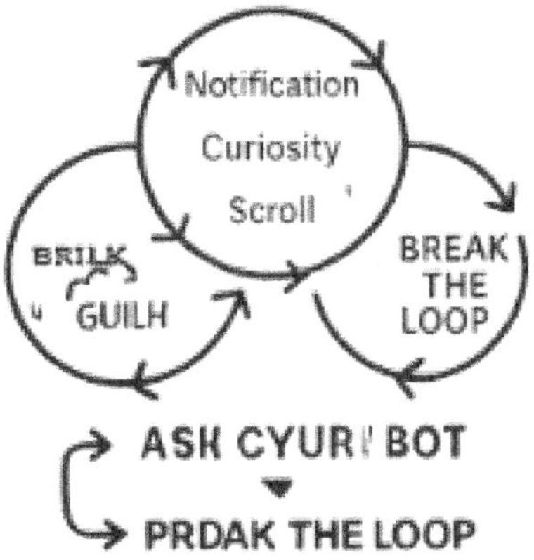

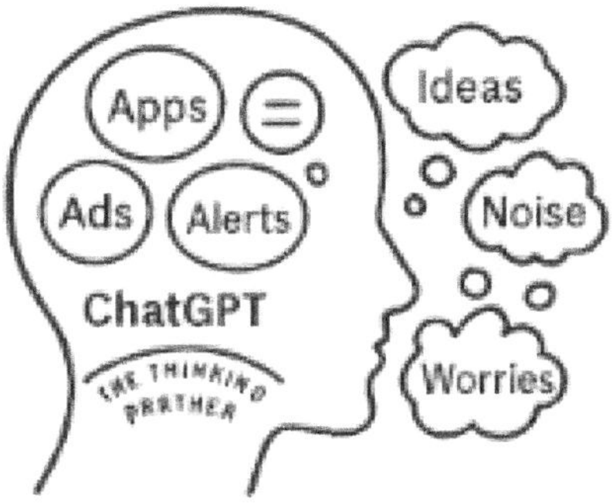

Each rung is one prompt closer to calm.

REBUILDING FOCUS

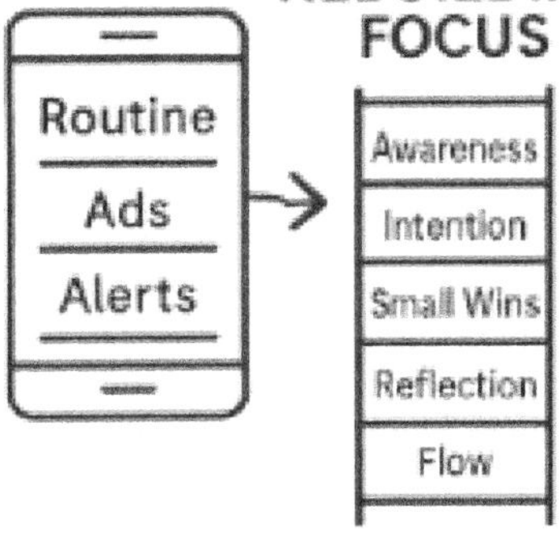

Each rung is one prompt closer to calm.

YOUR 24 HOURS OF ATTENTION

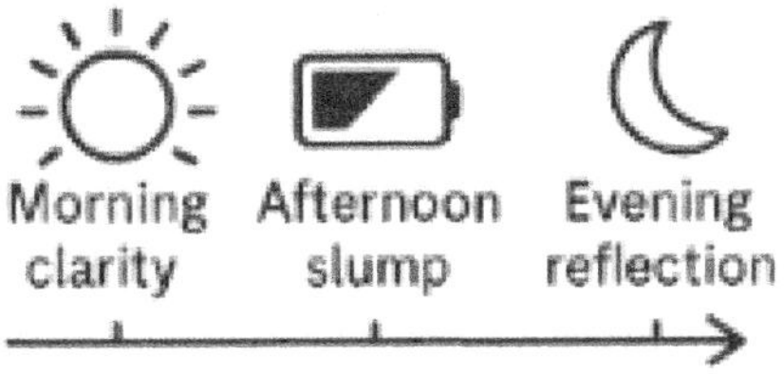

When does your mind feel sharpst?

What time do you lose focus most often?

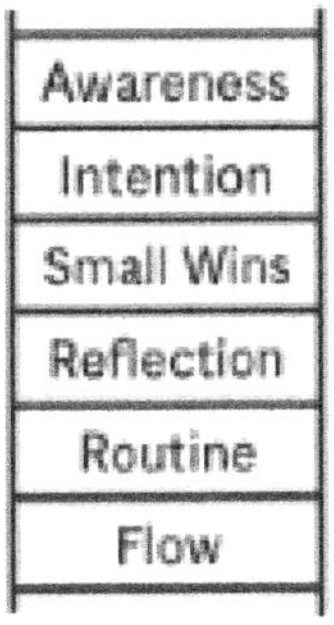

Easily Win Back Your Focus with ChatGPT

Focus Bot: Tiny Prompts for a Distracted World

Conversations for Clarity, Calm and Control in the Age of ChatGPT

We live in a world built to steal your attention. Every ping, post, and notification is designed to keep you scrolling.
Focus has become the new luxury—and distraction the default.

Focus is the cure for our world.
But not the kind that demands silence, rigid schedules, or dopamine detoxes.
The cure is awareness-and awareness begins with conversation.

Focus Bot shows you how to rebuild your attention one micro-moment at a time. Using the power of **ChatGPT as your thinking partner**, you'll learn to slow down, see clearly, and act intentionally.

No pills. No planners. No endless apps. Just use quick prompts to help you retrain your mind to choose focus over noise.

Inside You'll Discover:

• Simple daily ChatGPT prompts that restore clarity and control
• Real-world examples of "focus rewiring" in work, creativity, and relationships
• A 30-day challenge for rebuilding attention through guided reflection
• Why multitasking kills memory- and what to do instead
• How to transform your phone from a distraction device into a digital coach

Technology isn't the enemy. It's the tool.
The difference is how you use it.

Focus Bot is your guide to turning AI into an ally- one that listens, reflects, and helps you reclaim the part of yourself that endless scrolling forgot.

Introduction - Why This Book Exists

The world is louder than it has ever been.
Every ping, post, and pop-up wants a piece of your mind.

You wake up, grab your phone, and before your feet touch the floor, you've already spent your first thoughts on someone else's agenda.

You scroll.
You skim.
You swipe.
Repeat.

And by the time you sit down to work, the focus you needed most is already gone.
It's not your fault.

Your brain wasn't designed for this kind of overload. We are wired for patterns, not pressure, yet change now moves faster than our biology can adapt.

Every week brings new tools, new alerts, and new rules to follow. No wonder we feel behind before the day begins. This book isn't about blaming technology. It's about learning to partner with it.

Why Focus Now

Focus has become rare and fragile.

- We stand in line at Starbucks and can't go fifteen seconds without checking a phone.
- We open a tab for work and end up reading about someone else's vacation.
- We sit down to write but our brain whispers, "Maybe check your email first."

The attention crisis is real.

It's not just about distraction - it's about disconnection from our goals, creativity, and peace of mind.

If you can teach your brain to pause before reacting, you can rewrite how you think, work, and live.

Why Focus Became a Crisis

For most of human history, attention was shaped by the natural world. We focused on what moved, what fed us, or what might harm us. Today, that same survival wiring faces thousands of digital signals every hour.

Studies show that the average human attention span has dropped from about 12 seconds in 2000 to around 8 seconds today - shorter than a goldfish.

Teachers report that students now struggle to stay engaged for even 10 minutes. One national survey found that nearly one in five children has been evaluated for ADHD or similar conditions.

Adults aren't far behind. Prescriptions for focus-related medications have more than doubled in the past decade. Walk into any pharmacy or scroll through Amazon and you'll find capsules, gummies, and powders promising sharper memory and faster thinking. Focus has become a supplement, a subscription, even a stimulant.

That tells us something powerful: people are desperate to feel present again.

But the real problem isn't chemical - it's cognitive. Our brains are exhausted from managing too much input and too little reflection. We're losing not only our focus but our ability to notice what matters.

That's where this book comes in.

Instead of another pill, timer, or planner, you're going to learn a skill: how to use conversation itself as medicine for the mind.

When you engage with your Focus Bot, you practice awareness, not avoidance. You rebuild attention through curiosity, reflection, and consistent dialogue with a tool that helps you think instead of react.

Now that you understand what created this crisis, the next section shows you how to use this book and make ChatGPT your daily focus partner.

Why This Book Is Different

You've read the focus books. You've tried the planners, the timers, the detox apps. Most tell you to unplug and go offline.

That's not realistic.

You can't hide from the modern world, but you can learn to live inside it with clarity and control.

This book introduces something new - your own personal thinking partner, ChatGPT.

The Quiet UX Principle

In my work as a designer and educator, I've seen how much our tools shape our thinking.

Quiet UX means creating technology that serves attention rather than stealing it:

- A clear screen
- Fewer choices
- Gentle cues that guide rather than demand

Your Focus Bot works the same way. It's not here to flood you with noise - it's here to filter.

When you slow down and talk with your Bot, you're designing a quieter interface for your mind. You're choosing to shape technology around human rhythm instead of letting it shape you.

Chapter 1: The Foundations of Focus

The Attention Myth –

Why Multitasking Kills Memory and Creativity

You've been told multitasking makes you efficient.

That's a lie.

Science shows that every time you switch tasks, your brain burns energy reorienting itself. Psychologists call it "context switching," and it can cut your productivity by nearly 40%.

When you answer emails while half-listening to a meeting or scroll while watching a show, you're not doing two things. You're doing one thing badly, twice.

Your mind works best when it can sink in, not when it's asked to sprint in circles. Focus is not about discipline - it's about design. When you remove distractions, your brain stops sprinting and starts creating.

Prompt Practice
"Focus Bot, describe one time today when I tried to do too many things at once. What did it cost me?"

---

2. Your Digital Mind - How Devices Hijack Dopamine

Every ping, post, and pop-up trains your brain to crave the next hit.
The same neurotransmitter that motivates you to chase real goals - dopamine - is being spent on micro-rewards like likes, views, and notifications.

Tech companies have learned how to shape attention like clay. That's why your phone feels impossible to ignore. It's not weakness; it's wiring.

The problem isn't the device - it's the design. Every swipe, every buzz, every "new message" banner is engineered to remind your brain: *something better might be coming.*

Focus Bot helps you take that power back. When you use prompts to slow down, you retrain your dopamine system to release that same satisfaction from clarity instead of chaos.

Prompt Practice
"Focus Bot, help me identify three apps that drain my energy. How could I use them differently this week?"

---

3. Meet Your Bot - How to Personalize ChatGPT as Your Accountability Partner

Most people open ChatGPT and type a question. They close the tab the moment they get an answer. ***That's not partnership.***

This book teaches you to use ChatGPT as a **thinking partner** - a mirror that helps you slow

down, reflect, and reset.
When you talk to your Bot, you build a record of your focus story. It learns your tone, your goals, and your friction points.

Over time, it becomes your **accountability partner** - a private coach that helps you track attention, build habits, and reframe the day.

Here's how to start:

- Name your Bot. (You can call it "Focus Bot" or something that feels friendly.)
- Keep one thread open for your focus work.
- Use it daily, even briefly. Small conversations compound into awareness.

You'll begin to notice patterns: when your attention fades, what triggers distraction, and what recharges you.

Prompt Practice
"Focus Bot, what time of day do I seem most alert? What patterns do you notice in my energy?"

4. Tiny Prompts, Big Rewires - Why Micro-Habits Outperform Big Goals

Most people fail at focus because they set giant goals - "I'll work for four straight hours" or "I'll quit social media." Then life happens.

Micro-habits win because they meet you where you are.
You don't need to overhaul your brain. You just need one clear decision at a time.

That's why Focus Bot uses **micro-prompts** - tiny, repeatable questions that train attention gently instead of demanding willpower.
Each prompt rewires a single pathway in your brain, reinforcing calm awareness instead of autopilot reaction.

Focus isn't about fighting distraction. It's about noticing it sooner.

Prompt Practice
"Focus Bot, help me describe the moment today

when I lost concentration. What was I feeling, doing, or avoiding?"

How to Talk to Your Bot

You don't need to be a tech expert to use ChatGPT.
You only need curiosity and a few minutes of honesty.

Your Bot is not an app you "use."
It's a conversation partner - a thinking mirror that works best when you talk to it like a real person.

Start a Conversation

- Open ChatGPT (or any AI chat tool you prefer).
- 1. Type your question or use the **microphone icon** to dictate your message. You can pause, record. You don't have to record in just one take. You can keep

adding more until you are done. And you can add screenshots or attach files to help show your chatbot what you are talking about. You can speak naturally. Full sentences are not required.

- 2. Then, click the up arrow.

Example:
"Focus Bot, I can't seem to stay on task today. Ask me three questions that might help."

The Bot will respond in seconds. Read what it says, then reply.

You can keep going as long as the exchange helps you think more clearly.

Don't Worry About Grammar

Dictation isn't perfect - and it doesn't have to be.
Your Bot understands the spirit of what you're saying, even if a word is misheard or punctuation is off.
Think of it as a conversation with a good friend who listens between the lines.

Save What Matters

You can take a **screenshot** of any useful conversation or copy-paste it into your notes.
Some readers like to keep a digital folder labeled *Focus Chats* - others prefer to print a few pages for reflection.
You can even upload a file or photo if your platform allows it, and your Bot can help you organize or analyze it.

Stay Present

When you speak to your Bot, you're not multitasking - you're focusing.
You're training your attention to stay with one question, one idea, one emotion at a time.
That's where clarity begins.

Try It Now

Prompt Practice:
"Focus Bot, help me understand why I lose focus when I multitask. Ask me three simple questions to trace what happens in my mind."

Read the reply, reflect, and respond.
That's the rhythm of focus - one thoughtful exchange at a time.

Science Snapshot: How We Lost Our Focus

- Studies show the average attention span has dropped from **2½ minutes in 2004 to**

less than 47 seconds on digital devices today.

- Teenagers check their phones **over 100 times per day** on average.
- Diagnoses of ADHD and anxiety have risen sharply, especially among youth raised in digital-first environments.
- Companies now sell "focus gummies," "concentration teas," and even **prescription digital therapeutics** - proof that we've medicalized distraction.

The goal of this book is not to shame that reality. It's to rebuild the part of your brain that still remembers what stillness feels like.

Prompt Practice: Reflection Before Moving On

"Focus Bot, how do I usually react when I lose focus? What would it look like to pause before I react next time?"

Write down what you notice.
That's your first real exercise in attention.

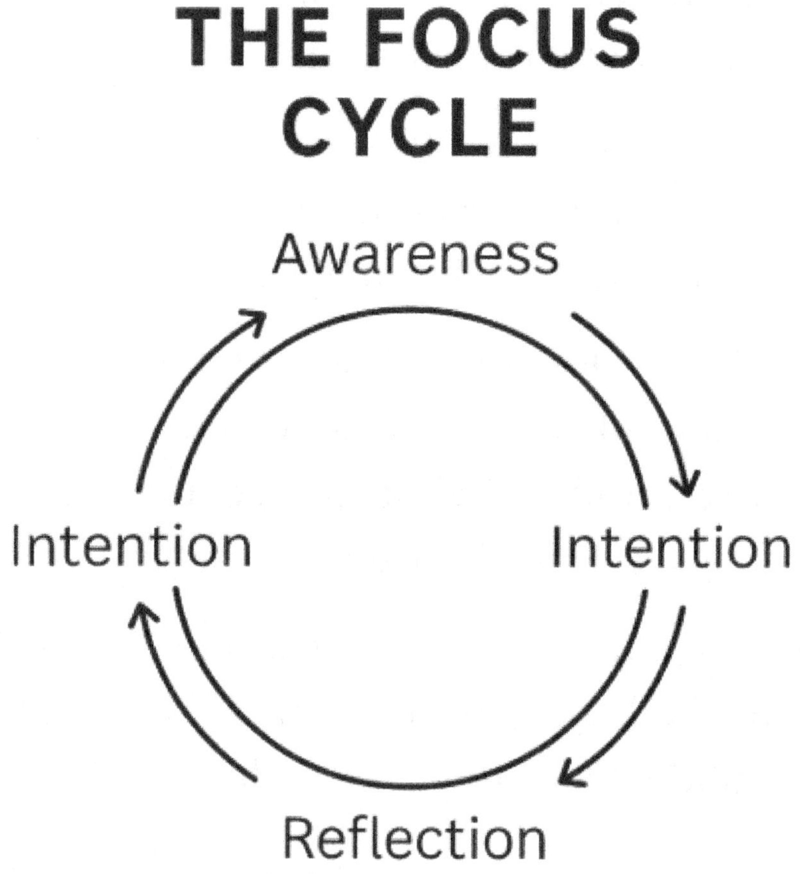

Focus Foundations Wrap-Up

You've seen what's really stealing your attention: multitasking myths, dopamine loops, and the constant digital pull that rewires how we think. You've also met your new ally - your **Focus Bot** -

and learned how small, consistent conversations can retrain your brain to slow down and choose what matters.

Here's what to remember:

- **You can't out-focus your environment.**
  To change your mind, you must change your inputs.
- **Attention is energy.**
  Every click or scroll spends a little of it. Start noticing where it goes.
- **Micro-prompts beat macro-plans.**
  Big systems fail because they demand perfection. Small questions work because they build awareness.
- **Your Bot is not Google.**
  It's your reflection partner. The goal isn't faster answers - it's slower thinking.

Reflection Prompt:

Ask your Bot —

"What moments today felt the noisiest, and what one choice could make tomorrow feel quieter?"

Then write down the response.
That's your first signal of awareness, the muscle this book will keep strengthening.

Quick Challenge:
Try one "focus fast" before Chapter 2. For the next 24 hours, pick one activity - eating, walking, or checking messages - and do it without multitasking. Notice what changes.

Get Real: Check Your Focus

Before you can fix a problem, you have to see it clearly.
Pick up your phone - yes, the one that's stealing your focus - and open your Screen Time or Digital Wellbeing settings.

How many hours were you on your phone today?

How many times did you pick it up?

Which apps took the most time?

Write it down.

This is your starting line. You can't change what you don't measure. Tell your bot to help you monitor it over the next month. Then you will have concrete evidence of where you started and how you improved.

Focus Bot prompt:

"Focus Bot, what surprised me most about my screen time today? What's one habit I can change this week to start taking back control?"

Chapter 2: 30 Days to a Clearer Mind

Why 30 Days?

Focus is a muscle, not a mood.
It doesn't appear overnight - it strengthens through small daily practice.

These next 30 days will show you how to retrain your attention one prompt at a time. Each day will include:

- A short idea or story to read
- A **Focus Bot prompt** to explore
- One small action that moves your mind toward clarity

You don't have to do it perfectly every day. The only goal is to keep showing up. Every short conversation with your Bot is a rep in your mental gym.

How to Use This Section

1. **Start anywhere.** The days are numbered, not dated. Skip ahead or circle back.
2. **Write with your Bot, not for it.** You're not journaling. You're dialoguing.
3. **Keep it short.** Five minutes of reflection beats an hour of rumination.
4. **Notice patterns.** What repeats? What drains? What does it restore?
5. **End each session with calm.** Breathe, stretch, or step outside. The goal is not output - it's awareness.

Focus Bot Prompt to Begin:
"Focus Bot, what do I most need more clarity about this month - my time, my priorities, or my peace of mind?"

Structure for Each Day

Each of the 30 days will follow this pattern:

Day Title (Theme)

A two-sentence overview that introduces the idea

Read: A short reflection (100–150 words)
Ask Your Bot: A practical ChatGPT prompt
Try This: A one-line action or experiment
Note It: A short reflection space (can be blank or with a guiding question)

30 Days to a Clearer Mind

Why 30 Days?

Focus is a muscle, not a mood.
It doesn't appear overnight. It strengthens through small daily practice.

Over the next 30 days, this retraining will focus your attention on one prompt at a time. Each day includes:

- A short idea to read
- A **Focus Bot prompt** to explore

- One small action that moves your mind toward clarity

The goal isn't perfection. It's awareness.
Every five-minute conversation with your Bot is a step toward a quieter mind.

How to Use This Section

1. Start anywhere. The days are numbered, not dated.
2. Write with your Bot, not for it. You're not journaling. You're dialoguing.
3. Keep it short. Five minutes of reflection beats an hour of overthinking.
4. Notice patterns. What repeats? What does it restore?
5. End each session with calm. Breathe, stretch, or step outside.

Prompt to Begin:

"Focus Bot, what do I most need clarity about

this month - my time, my priorities, or my peace of mind?"

---

30 Days to a Clearer Mind

Day 1: Begin Again

Every focus journey starts with a pause. You can't rebuild your attention if your mind is already racing.
Take five minutes to breathe before you open your next app or tab. You've already started.

Ask Your Bot:
"Focus Bot, what's the first thought I had this morning? Did it help me start the day or scatter my mind?"

Try This: Turn off one non-essential notification today.

Day 2: The Noise Audit

Your brain has limited bandwidth. Each alert, conversation, and worry takes up space.
Today, notice what fills your mind - and what deserves to stay.

Ask Your Bot:
"Focus Bot, what noises, habits, or voices distract me most often?"

Try This: Choose one kind of noise to silence for a day - a group chat, an email alert, or a random scroll.

Day 3: The Dopamine Loop

The scroll feels good for a reason. Each swipe releases dopamine, your brain's "anticipation" chemical.
The secret is not quitting dopamine, but redirecting it toward focus and satisfaction.

Ask Your Bot:
"Focus Bot, what simple task gives me a small but real sense of reward?"

Try This: After finishing one focused task, take a slow breath and say, "That was enough."

Day 4: Clear the Desk, Clear the Mind

Visual clutter creates mental clutter. A crowded desk, desktop, or inbox keeps your mind in half-finished mode.

Ask Your Bot:
"Focus Bot, what physical or digital space needs to breathe today?"

Try This: Declutter one small area you look at daily. Leave it empty for 24 hours.

Day 5: Your Attention Is Currency

Every click and scroll is a transaction. Someone profits from your distraction.
When you notice your attention leaking, pause and remember that it's worth something.

Ask Your Bot:
"Focus Bot, where did I spend my attention today? Was it worth it?"

Try This: Track how many times you unlock your phone before lunch.

Day 6: Focus Fatigue

You can't focus forever. Your brain runs on cycles. The trick is not to push harder, but to rest smarter.

Ask Your Bot:
"Focus Bot, when does my energy drop most often each day?"

Try This: Schedule your hardest task one hour before that slump begins.

Day 7: The 5-Minute Rule

Most procrastination isn't fear of work - it's fear of starting. Promise yourself you'll focus for just five minutes.
Momentum will do the rest.

Ask Your Bot:
"Focus Bot, what task am I avoiding right now? Can I give it five minutes?"

Try This: Start a timer for five minutes. When it rings, decide if you want to keep going.

Day 8: Design Your Flow Zone

Find your personal focus recipe - the music, time, and setting where you feel most alive.

Ask Your Bot:
"Focus Bot, describe my ideal focus zone. What does it sound, feel, or look like?"

Try This: Recreate one small part of that environment today.

Day 9: One Tab at a Time

Every open tab is a tug on your mind.
When everything is visible, nothing gets done.

Ask Your Bot:
"Focus Bot, which open tabs or projects represent unfinished thoughts?"

Try This: Close them all. Open only the one you're working on.

Day 10: Focus Foods

Your brain burns about 20% of your body's energy.
What you eat fuels or fogs your attention.

Ask Your Bot:
"Focus Bot, how do I feel one hour after my usual lunch?"

Try This: Replace one processed snack with water or fruit and notice the change.

Day 11: Guard the Mornings

The first 90 minutes of your day decide your tone.
Don't donate them to chaos.

Ask Your Bot:
"Focus Bot, what's the first thing that deserves my focus tomorrow morning?"

Try This: Leave your phone off for the first 15 minutes after waking.

Day 12: The Single-Task Experiment

Doing one thing at a time feels slow - until you realize it's faster.

Ask Your Bot:
"Focus Bot, what's one task I could give my full attention to right now?"

Try This: For 20 minutes, do just that task. No switching. Notice how it feels.

Day 13: Tame the To-Do List

A list with 30 items is not a plan. It's a trap.
Shrink it to three priorities a day.

Ask Your Bot:
"Focus Bot, what are my top three most important actions today?"

Try This: Cross everything off until tomorrow.

Day 14: The Midday Reset

Halfway through the day, your mind starts to drift.
Reset instead of powering through.

Ask Your Bot:
"Focus Bot, what part of my day drains me most? What might restore me?"

Try This: Step outside for five minutes. No phone. Just light and air.

Day 15: Digital Boundaries

Focus needs fences.
Decide when you'll be online - and when you won't.

Ask Your Bot:
"Focus Bot, what digital boundary could protect my best hours?"

Try This: Create one "no-scroll zone" today.

Day 16: Emotional Clutter

Your thoughts can't settle if your emotions are unspoken.
Before work, name what you're feeling - even briefly.

Ask Your Bot:
"Focus Bot, what emotion is sitting closest to my attention today?"

Try This: Write one sentence that names it.
Then begin your work.

Day 17: Quiet Wins

Not every achievement needs applause.
Focus thrives in quiet progress.

Ask Your Bot:
"Focus Bot, what did I complete today that no one else noticed?"

Try This: Celebrate it privately. Let stillness be your reward.

Day 18: The Power of Stop

Pausing is an act of intelligence.
Stopping at the right time keeps you from burning out.

Ask Your Bot:
"Focus Bot, what could I stop doing today that no longer serves me?"

Try This: Say no to one small thing that drains your time.

Day 19: The Environment Reset

Every room trains your behavior.
If your desk whispers "scroll," change it.

Ask Your Bot:
"Focus Bot, how does my current workspace make me feel?"

Try This: Rearrange one small part of it to signal focus.

Day 20: The 2-Minute Mind

Small completions build confidence.
Finish something tiny to remind your brain that you can finish big.

Ask Your Bot:
"Focus Bot, what micro-task could I complete right now?"

Try This: Do it before you overthink it.

Day 21: The Social Scroll

You can't compare your behind-the-scenes to someone else's highlight reel.
Social media is not reality. It's advertising.

Ask Your Bot:
"Focus Bot, what emotions rise when I scroll? Inspiration or envy?"

Try This: Skip social media for one full evening.

Day 22: Music for Flow

Sound shapes focus.
Try instrumental music, white noise, or silence until you find your groove.

Ask Your Bot:
"Focus Bot, what sounds help me think best?"

Try This: Curate a short "flow playlist" for your next deep work session.

Day 23: The Power of Routine

Your brain loves rhythm.
Routine isn't boring - it's freeing.

Ask Your Bot:
"Focus Bot, what part of my day feels most stable? How can I build on that?"

Try This: Anchor one new habit to something you already do daily.

Day 24: Sleep, the Silent Multiplier

You can't outsmart exhaustion.
Focus begins the night before.

Ask Your Bot:
"Focus Bot, what's one thing keeping me from deeper sleep?"

Try This: Turn off all screens 30 minutes before bed.

Day 25: Focus and Movement

Your body teaches your brain how to focus.
A short walk resets memory and mood.

Ask Your Bot:
"Focus Bot, when was the last time I truly moved with intention?"

Try This: Walk five minutes without your phone and breathe deeply.

Day 26: Reclaiming Boredom

Boredom used to be fertile ground for ideas.
Now we fill every gap with noise.

Ask Your Bot:
"Focus Bot, when was the last time I let myself be bored?"

Try This: Wait in silence instead of pulling out your phone.

Day 27: Reconnecting with Purpose

Distraction thrives in the absence of meaning.
Clarity returns when you remember why you care.

Ask Your Bot:
"Focus Bot, why does my work matter to me?"

Try This: Write one sentence that answers it. Keep it near your workspace.

Day 28: The Energy Audit

You can't manage time without managing energy.
Notice what fuels you - and what drains you.

Ask Your Bot:
"Focus Bot, who or what gives me the most energy lately?"

Try This: Spend more time there tomorrow.

Day 29: Attention and Gratitude

Gratitude is a focus pointed inward.
It shifts your brain from scarcity to sufficiency.

Ask Your Bot:
"Focus Bot, what small thing am I grateful for today that I almost missed?"

Try This: Say it out loud. Once.

Day 30: Clarity Is a Practice

Focus isn't a destination. It's a rhythm you return to.
The clearer your mind becomes, the more creative space you reclaim.

Ask Your Bot:
"Focus Bot, how has my attention changed over the last 30 days?"

Try This: Choose one practice from this month to carry forward.

Closing Reflection:

You don't need to escape technology to find peace.
You just need to use it as a partner instead of a parasite.
Your Bot isn't replacing your mind. It's helping you meet it again - with calm, curiosity, and clarity.

30-Day Reflection and Wrap-Up

You've just completed 30 days of focus training.
You've practiced noticing your attention instead of chasing it.
You've learned to pause, breathe, and ask questions that bring your thoughts back home.

Now it's time to reflect.

Take a few minutes with your Bot, or with pen and paper, and answer these simple questions.
There's no right or wrong answer. Just honesty.

Reflect on Your Journey

1. Which day's exercise challenged you the most?
2. What was the moment when you almost gave up - and what helped you continue?
3. Which prompt still echoes in your mind?
4. What surprised you about your own habits or patterns?
5. When did you feel the calmest?

Prompt Practice:
"Focus Bot, what did I learn about my own attention this month? What changed about how I see time, focus, or rest?"

Track the Shift

Look back at your first day.
Has your relationship with distraction changed?
Do you feel less reactive, even a little more in control?
Those small differences are evidence of growth - the rewiring of your mind toward clarity.

You've learned that attention isn't something you have or lose.
It's something you practice.
And practice doesn't end here.

Next Step

Now that you've built awareness, it's time to design systems that protect it.
In the next chapter, you'll learn how to turn daily focus into a sustainable routine - how to make clarity automatic instead of accidental.

Keep your Focus Bot open.
Your next conversation will begin a new kind of calm.

Chapter 2 Summary - What You've Learned

Over the last 30 days, you proved that focus can be rebuilt in small, consistent steps.
You learned to:

- Notice when your attention drifts and bring it back without judgment

- Use short prompts to think instead of scroll
- Turn your Bot into a mirror that helps you see patterns, not problems
- Replace pressure with presence - one mindful pause at a time
- Recognize that quiet isn't weakness; it's where your best ideas grow

Each five-minute session trains your brain to choose clarity over chaos.
You now have evidence that your focus can improve - and that technology, when used intentionally, can support calm rather than noise.

- If you completed even half the exercises, you're already rewiring your attention.
- The goal isn't perfection; it's awareness. Awareness is what keeps your focus alive.

Moving Forward

The next step is structure.
You've built awareness of your habits - now you'll design systems that protect your focus automatically.

Chapter 3: Building Focus Systems

Designing a Life That Protects Your Attention

Focus doesn't last by accident.
It lasts because you've built structures around it.

You don't rise to the level of your motivation.
You fall to the level of your systems.

This chapter is about creating the quiet scaffolding that supports clear thinking every day - even when the world around you gets loud again.

Why Systems Matter

Motivation fades fast. Energy shifts hour to hour.
But a good system doesn't depend on willpower.
It's there when you forget, when you're tired, when life gets messy.

Systems keep you from starting over.
They remove choice in the best way - not to

restrict you, but to free your brain from constant decision-making.

Ask Your Bot:
"Focus Bot, what part of my day feels hardest to control? How could a system help me here instead of pure effort?"

The Four Pillars of a Focus System

1. **Environment** - Your surroundings whisper cues all day. Design them to say "start," not "scroll."
2. **Energy** - Know your natural rhythm. Protect your peak hours like money in the bank.
3. **Routine** - Build repeatable sequences that make focus automatic.
4. **Recovery** - Schedule rest as deliberately as work. Fatigue is the fastest thief of attention.

Prompt Practice:
"Focus Bot, which of these four pillars feels weakest in my life right now? What's one small way to strengthen it?"

---

1. Environment: Make Focus the Default

You can't concentrate in chaos.
Your brain records every open loop - every pile, tab, and notification.

Small shifts create big calm:

- Keep your workspace visually simple.
- Use one browser for work, one for personal browsing.
- Place tools within reach, distractions out of sight.
- Add one sensory cue for focus - a candle, playlist, or specific chair.

Try This:
Create a "Focus Corner" - a clean, defined spot that tells your brain it's time to think.

---

2. Energy: Match Your Mind to the Clock

Most people work *against* their natural rhythm. Notice when you feel most alert - morning, midday, or night - and schedule hard thinking there.

Your low-energy blocks are for routine tasks, not deep creation.

Ask Your Bot:
"Focus Bot, when during the day do I feel most mentally alive? What task deserves that energy tomorrow?"

Try This:
Protect your best two hours. Guard them from meetings and noise.

---

3. Routine: Automation for the Mind

Repetition is relief.
When you do something at the same time every day, your brain stops negotiating about it.

Simple routines build trust with yourself:

- Begin the day with one question instead of a scroll.
- Set a timer for the first 20 minutes of work.
- Take the same short walk at the same time every afternoon.

Prompt Practice:
"Focus Bot, what tiny daily habit could anchor my mornings in calm?"

---

4. Recovery: Rest Is Part of the System

True focus includes stopping.
If you push until you crash, your brain learns that concentration equals pain.

Rest teaches your nervous system safety - and safety is what allows deep work.

Protect recovery as fiercely as output:

- Short breaks every 90 minutes.
- Digital sunset one hour before bed.
- Something quiet but joyful each day - reading, drawing, music, prayer, silence.

Ask Your Bot:
"Focus Bot, what kind of rest actually restores me? What fake rest do I need to let go of?"

System Design in Action

Here's how these pieces work together.

Morning: quiet start, one clear task, phone still off.
Midday: energy audit, five-minute reset.
Evening: reflection prompt with your Bot, prepare tomorrow's workspace.

That's a focus system - a rhythm that holds you steady when the day pulls you off track.

Prompt Practice:
"Focus Bot, help me name my daily rhythm in three words. What do those words mean to me?"

Quick Checklist: Your Personal Focus Architecture

- I have a workspace that supports clarity
- I know my best focus hours
- I protect time for rest and renewal
- I use short prompts instead of long to-do lists
- I end each day with reflection instead of reaction

If you can check even three of these, you've built the beginnings of a sustainable focus system.

Chapter 3 Summary - Protecting the Quiet

A focused life isn't built by accident.
It's crafted through gentle, repeatable patterns

that keep your attention aligned with your values.

You now have the framework to stay steady when the world speeds up again.

In the next chapter, you'll learn how to **extend your focus outward** - how to lead, create, and connect without losing your calm core.

Chapter 4: Leading with Clarity

How to Stay Calm, Create Deeply, and Communicate Well in a Distracted World

Focus isn't only personal.

When you hold it, everyone around you feels it. Your calm becomes contagious.

This chapter shows how to carry that quiet strength into your work, relationships, and creative life.

You'll learn how to listen better, decide faster, and communicate in ways that invite focus instead of noise.

---

1. The Ripple Effect of Calm

Every meeting, classroom, and family dinner takes on the energy of its calmest person.

Be that person.
You don't need authority to lead - only attention.

When you stay centered, others match your rhythm.
You're teaching focus by example.

Ask Your Bot:
"Focus Bot, when do I lose my calm around others? What would it look like to keep my clarity in that moment?"

---

2. Communicating with Presence

Most people listen only long enough to reply.
Real leaders listen to understand.

Practical habits:

- Pause before responding.
- Repeat back what you heard.
- Ask one clarifying question before giving advice.

Presence turns every conversation into collaboration.

Prompt Practice:
"Focus Bot, help me phrase my next difficult conversation so that I sound calm and clear."

---

3. Creative Focus in Teams

Creativity dies in chaos.
The best ideas come from structured freedom - clear goals with room to explore.

Build creative focus systems:

- Define what "done" looks like.
- Limit brainstorming time.
- End meetings with one next step, not ten possibilities.

Ask Your Bot:
"Focus Bot, what question could help my team cut through noise and find one shared goal?"

---

4. The Quiet Leader

Leadership doesn't require volume.
It requires vision and steadiness.

Quiet leaders guide by clarity, not control.
They focus on outcomes, not ownership.

Try This:
Before your next meeting, set a silent intention:
I'm here to listen first.

---

5. Digital Etiquette for the Focused Era

Distraction multiplies when communication never ends.
Set boundaries that protect your clarity:

- Batch replies instead of living in your inbox.
- Use short, direct messages.
- Schedule "no-chat" hours for deep work.

Ask Your Bot:
"Focus Bot, how can I communicate boundaries at work without sounding distant?"

---

6. Focus and Empathy

Focus isn't selfish - it's a form of respect.
When you give someone your full attention, they feel seen.
That attention deepens connection more than any multitasking ever could.

Prompt Practice:
"Focus Bot, who in my life deserves more of my full attention this week?"

---

7. The Creative Core

Every artist, maker, or thinker needs protected time to create.
Guard it like sacred space.

You can't serve others if your own creative well is empty.

Try This:
Schedule one "quiet block" each week - no meetings, no messages, just your craft.

---

8. Decision Clarity

Indecision is a form of mental clutter.
A clear mind decides faster and regrets less.

Ask simple questions before saying yes:

- Does this align with my values?
- Will this matter in a month?
- What will I have to trade for it?

Ask Your Bot:
"Focus Bot, walk me through a decision I've been avoiding. Help me see the trade-offs clearly."

---

9. Teaching Focus Forward

If you mentor, parent, or teach, you're shaping the next generation's relationship with

attention.
Model calm curiosity.
Show that technology can be thoughtful, not frantic.

Prompt Practice:
"Focus Bot, how can I teach a child or student to focus without punishment - through example instead?"

10. Leading by Design

Your systems become invisible over time - that's how you know they work.
The leader's role is to keep refining them quietly.

At home, at work, in your creative life - design everything to make focus easy and distraction inconvenient.

Ask Your Bot:
"Focus Bot, what one change could make my environment feel calmer this week?"

Chapter 4 Summary - The Clarity Multiplier

When you stay centered, you multiply clarity for everyone around you.
Focus is leadership.
Listening is innovation.
Calm is power.

You've learned how to use your Bot not just for personal peace, but to build trust, collaboration, and creativity in every space you touch.

In the next chapter, you'll turn inward again - exploring how attention and emotion connect, and how to keep your focus alive even through stress and change.

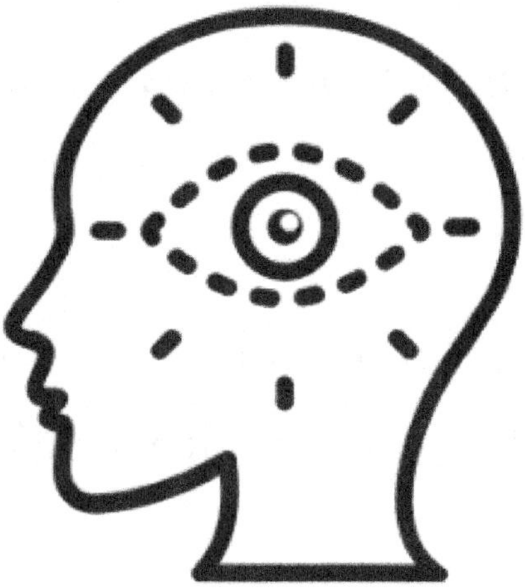

Chapter 5: Breaking the Loop

How to Rewire Your Attention Without the Pills, the Panic, or the Guilt

Let's be honest.
Most of us are addicted.
Not to our phones themselves, but to the feeling they create - that tiny rush when a message lights up the screen.

You're not weak. You're wired.
Your brain evolved to chase novelty and reward.
Now that same wiring meets a machine that never runs out of both.

The Dopamine Trap

Every swipe, ding, and buzz drops a trace of dopamine into your bloodstream.
That's the chemical of *anticipation*, not satisfaction.
It keeps you checking, waiting for the next spark.

The loop looks like this:
Cue ↠ Click ↠ Reward ↠ Repeat.

Your brain learns the rhythm until stillness feels wrong.
That's why focus drugs and supplements only numb the noise; they don't re-teach calm.
They stimulate the same chemical your phone already abuses.
They treat the symptom, not the system.

Science Behind the Loop

Yes - you are in many ways part of a grand experiment.
Your brain, your attention, and your devices form a trio designed for one thing: keeping you looking, scrolling, and waiting for the next hit.

- **The attention economy**

The phrase itself says it: companies don't sell apps. They sell *your attention*.

Your attention becomes a product. Every notification, every feed refresh, every new video is engineered to keep you there - because more time means more data, more ads, more profit.

- **Designed for addiction**

One study found that simply having your smartphone within reach (even if it's not in use) can lower available cognitive capacity.

Another research project showed that participants exposed to smartphone notifications had slower response times and weaker attentional control.

- **The reward loop**

Your brain is hard-wired for novelty and reward. When your phone gives you something new with minimal effort, the dopamine system lights up. Then it learns: *cue* ↠ *click* ↠ *reward.*

That loop becomes the default pattern of your attention system - not because you're lazy, but because you're living in a design built to hijack the impulse.

- **When you try to pause**

What happens when you try to calm that loop? One experiment found that blocking mobile internet access for 2 weeks improved attention spans in adults—the equivalent of "reversing 10 years of cognitive decline."

That's proof: it's not just a distraction, it's an adaptation. Your brain learned to live this way.

Why It Matters Here

If this were just about bad habits, you'd fix it with discipline.
But when your brain's chemistry and billions of lines of code work together to keep you hooked,

you need more than "just stop."
You need a plan that rewires how you respond.
That plan uses your Bot.
That plan uses awareness.
That plan uses structure - not punishment.

Prompt Practice:
"Focus Bot, how many times did I unlock my phone today before I told myself 'Just one minute'? What was I expecting to find?"

Why the Focus Pill Isn't Enough

Medications can help with true medical conditions, but for most people, they only mask the overload.

They sharpen attention for a while but never rebuild discipline.
You can't outsource self-awareness.
You have to retrain it.

That's what this chapter is about - learning how to quiet the chemical chase and rebuild your inner balance.

Ask Your Bot:
"Focus Bot, what am I usually avoiding when I reach for my phone? What emotion do I not want to feel right then?"

Step 1: Notice the Craving

The first step isn't quitting.
It's noticing.
Pause before you tap.
Ask yourself, *what am I expecting to find here?*
That moment of honesty breaks the reflex.

Try This:
The next time you reach for your phone, don't stop - just watch yourself do it.
Awareness alone begins the rewiring.

Step 2: Replace the Rush

The brain hates a vacuum.
When you remove a stimulus, fill it with something nourishing.
Movement, breath, art, sound, silence - anything that restores rather than excites.

Your Bot can help:

"Focus Bot, suggest three quick activities that give me calm energy instead of digital noise."

You'll discover small anchors that satisfy the same need without the crash.

Step 3: Rebuild Reward Pathways

Each time you finish a task without checking your phone, celebrate it.
Acknowledge the effort.
Tiny victories teach your brain that focus itself is rewarding.

Try This:
After twenty minutes of uninterrupted work,

stand up, stretch, and say out loud, "I did that." Your brain registers the pride as a new kind of dopamine hit - the healthy kind.

Step 4: Redesign Your Environment

Make distraction inconvenient and focus easy.
Keep chargers out of reach.
Set your phone to grayscale mode.
Move addictive apps to hidden folders.
Design your space to whisper calm.

Prompt Practice:
"Focus Bot, what small change to my workspace would make distraction less tempting?"

Step 5: Reconnect With Real Reward

At the core of every craving is a need - connection, meaning, validation.
When you meet those needs directly, the phone loses power.
Call someone. Step outside. Create something.

Pray.
That's real dopamine: earned, not injected.

Ask Your Bot:
"Focus Bot, what brings me joy that doesn't come from a screen?"

The New Chemistry of Calm

You can't medicate your way into peace.
You can practice your way there.
Each small pause, each mindful question, retrains the nervous system that's been hijacked by modern life.

Focus isn't just mental - it's chemical, physical, spiritual.
When you change your inputs, you change your brain.

Chapter 5 Summary - Freedom From the Loop

You don't need another pill, app, or detox.
You need awareness, structure, and the courage to face silence again.

You've learned how to:

- Identify the dopamine loop
- Replace empty rush with a real reward
- Redesign your space for calm
- Use your Bot as a partner in rewiring attention

This is how you heal your focus - by giving your brain the calm it forgot it loved.

Chapter 6: The Chemistry of Calm

How to Train a Peaceful Mind in a Busy World

You don't find calm. You build it.
Just like focus, peace is a system - a series of small choices that teach your body it's safe to relax.

The world rewards urgency, not presence.
But your nervous system can't live in high alert forever.
To focus well, you must first learn how to *come down.*

The Two Brains in One Body

You have two operating modes:

- The **Stress System** - fight, flight, scroll, react.
- The **Calm System** - breathe, reflect, respond, restore.

Most people live in the stress system without realizing it.
Constant alerts and deadlines keep adrenaline dripping into your bloodstream.
Your heart races. Your thoughts scatter. You forget to exhale.

The calm system isn't weak.
It's strategic.
It's the setting where you can think deeply, create freely, and connect fully.

Ask Your Bot:
"Focus Bot, how does my body tell me when I'm in stress mode? What could I do to signal safety instead?"

Step 1: Interrupt the Stress Cycle

When you feel the rush of tension, your brain believes there's danger - even if it's just an email.
To switch from reaction to reflection, you need a short, physical cue.

Try one of these:

- Breathe in for four counts, out for six.
- Place your hand on your chest and say, "I'm safe."
- Look around and name three calm things you see.

These actions send a signal to your brain: *Stand down. We're okay.*

Prompt Practice:
"Focus Bot, give me three ways to calm my nervous system when I feel overwhelmed."

Step 2: Redefine Productivity

Peaceful people get more done because they waste less energy on panic.
The myth of "always on" work keeps you wired and tired.
You're not lazy when you rest - you're strategic.

Make recovery part of your focus plan.
Schedule breaks like appointments.
Protect quiet time like revenue.

Ask Your Bot:
"Focus Bot, help me design a daily rhythm that balances focus and rest."

Step 3: Rewire the Reward

When you stop chasing crisis, your brain panics at first.
It misses the rush of urgency.
But calm creates its own chemistry - serotonin and oxytocin, the compounds of contentment and trust.

You can train your brain to crave this quieter high through small rituals:

- Warm light in the morning.
- Slow music while you work.
- Ending each day with one line of gratitude.

These are not luxuries; they're rewiring tools.

Try This:
Whisper, "This is enough," three times a day - morning, noon, and night. Watch what changes.

Step 4: Build Your Calm Kit

Your nervous system learns through repetition. When you create a set of calm triggers, your body remembers how to return to peace.

Your Calm Kit might include:

- A playlist that steadies your breathing
- A scent that signals rest
- One sentence that reminds you who you are
- A space where no screens are allowed

Prompt Practice:
"Focus Bot, help me make a short list of objects, sounds, or phrases that help me feel grounded."

Step 5: Practice Inner Kindness

You can't bully yourself into peace.
Self-criticism keeps you in fight mode.
Gentleness builds stamina.

When you speak kindly to yourself, your nervous system relaxes - and your focus improves.
Replace "I'm behind" with "I'm learning."
Replace "I messed up" with "I noticed."

Ask Your Bot:
"Focus Bot, help me rewrite one negative thought into something compassionate but still true."

The Science of Stillness

Calm isn't passive.
It's an active neurological state where your prefrontal cortex - the thinking part of your brain - comes back online.
That's when you plan clearly, solve creatively, and communicate without panic.

Meditation, prayer, art, nature - all activate this same system.
The form doesn't matter.
The feeling of safety does.

Try This: The 60-Second Reset

Whenever you feel scattered:

1. Exhale slowly.
2. Drop your shoulders.
3. Ask your Bot one question that matters right now.
4. Read the answer.
5. Breathe again.

It's that simple - a one-minute nervous system reboot.

Chapter 6 Summary - Calm Is Contagious

You've learned that calm isn't the absence of motion; it's movement with awareness.
When you train peace, your mind becomes your ally again.
When you choose quiet, you choose power.

Now that you can regulate your energy, the next step is to apply that clarity outward - to your creativity, your work, and your purpose.

Chapter 7: Creative Flow

Turning Focus Into Art, Work and Meaning

Creativity is the reward for attention.
When your mind is quiet, your ideas finally have room to breathe.
This chapter is a studio—part workshop, part reflection space, part spark.

You've built calm.
Now it's time to use it.

Focus isn't just for discipline - it's the doorway to imagination.
When your mind finally quiets, your creativity wakes up.

The Silence Before the Spark

All great ideas begin in stillness.
Mozart called it the space "between the notes."
Writers, painters, inventors - they all learn to trust the pause.

We lose that space when our attention is scattered.
The phone steals the silence where insight grows.

Today, we rebuild it.
Not by forcing ideas, but by *inviting* them.

Reflection:
Think of a time when an idea arrived out of nowhere - in the shower, while driving, or watching the sky.
That wasn't luck. It was flow. Your mind was finally quiet enough to listen.

Exercise 1: Create a Quiet Ritual

Before any creative work - writing, designing, problem-solving - give yourself a short ritual. Something that signals, *I'm entering the flow zone.*

Examples:

- A cup of tea poured slowly

- A single candle lit
- A favorite playlist or stretch

Keep it under two minutes. The shorter the ritual, the stronger the association.

Then start. Don't plan - just begin.

The Myth of Inspiration

People think creativity is a bolt of lightning. It's not. It's a pulse - a rhythm you can train.

When you create a calm environment, your brain's default network lights up.
That's the system that connects random thoughts into new ideas.
Focus doesn't kill creativity; it frees it.

Story Break: The Artist's Window

When I was teaching design, one of my students told me she kept moving her desk around, chasing the "perfect light."

After weeks, she realized it wasn't the light she needed. It was *permission to sit still long enough for the light to move.*

Flow happens when you stop rearranging and start receiving.

Exercise 2: The 20-Minute Flow Test

Set a timer for 20 minutes.
Pick one task - painting, typing, cleaning, or organizing.
Tell yourself you don't have to finish. You only have to stay in it.

At minute 15, you'll notice something shift.
Your brain will stop negotiating.
That's flow - attention that feels like ease.

When the timer rings, stop.
Don't push. Let satisfaction settle in.

That's how creative stamina is built - small, steady, repeatable sessions.

The Three Layers of Flow

1. **The Entry** - distraction drops, curiosity rises.
2. **The Deep Zone** - time disappears, energy expands.
3. **The Glow** - when you stop, you feel both calm and alive.

You can't live in flow all day, but you can design for it daily.
The goal isn't to chase the feeling; it's to make it visit often.

Reflection Break

Write down three activities where you naturally lose track of time.
That's your creative compass.
Do one of them tomorrow - even for ten minutes.

Flow rewards consistency, not talent.

The Energy Exchange

Creative flow is not always peaceful.
Sometimes it's messy, emotional, uncomfortable.
That's part of the process - your brain reorganizing information into new patterns.

The secret is not to escape that tension.
It's to stay long enough to see what it's trying to show you.

When frustration hits, say quietly:
"This is part of the work."
Because it is.

Exercise 3: The Three-Sentence Story

You can use this for writing, journaling, or problem-solving.
Ask your mind to tell a story in exactly three sentences.

Example:

"I wanted to rest, but my thoughts wouldn't stop.
Then I turned off the noise and listened to the hum of the world.
The answer was there all along."

Three sentences. No editing. Just flow.

The Creative Equation

Focus × Curiosity = Flow.
Flow × Meaning = Fulfillment.

When you work with presence, even small projects become sacred.
That's what this chapter is training you to see - that the ordinary can be extraordinary when your mind is clear.

Closing Reflection

You've trained focus.
You've practiced calm.

Now you're remembering how to create from clarity, not chaos.

The next time you sit down to work, whisper:
"I don't need to hurry. I need to listen."

That's how art begins.
That's how meaning returns.

SECTION 1: The Flow State

When you create, time disappears.
That's not magic; it's focus at work.

Scientists call it *transient hypofrontality*—the part of your brain that doubts and delays goes offline.

You stop managing your thoughts and start moving with them.

Try This: The Two-Minute Warm-Up
Write, sketch, or build something small for two

minutes without stopping.
Don't edit. Don't plan.
Just move.

Ask Your Bot:

"Focus Bot, what kind of work makes me lose track of time? What does that say about the way my brain loves to focus?"

SECTION 2: Your Creative Energy Map

Not all creativity looks like art.
It can be problem-solving, gardening, coding, or cooking.
You have patterns—times, textures, and tools that ignite ideas.

Worksheet:

- Best time of day for creative flow:

  ____

  ____

- Environments that inspire me:

  ____

  ____

- People or sounds that drain me:

  ____

  ____

- One symbol that represents my creative rhythm:

  ____

  ____

Ask Your Bot:

"Focus Bot, describe my creative style in three words. How could I use that awareness to plan my day better?"

SECTION 3: Interruptions as Information

Every distraction has a message.
When you drift, it's often because something inside you is bored, anxious, or craving novelty.
Don't fight the drift—decode it.

Prompt Practice:

"Focus Bot, what might my last distraction be trying to tell me about my energy or emotions?"

Then decide: fix the root, not the symptom.

SECTION 4: The Creative Ritual

Focus thrives on ritual.
Even artists who love chaos have anchors: same coffee mug, same playlist, same walk before work.
Rituals cue the brain: *now we make.*

Design Your Own:

1. Choose a starting signal (sound, scent, or light).
2. Choose a closing signal (clean desk, stretch, or short note to self).
3. Repeat daily for one week.

Ask Your Bot:

"Focus Bot, help me design a five-minute ritual that tells my brain it's time to create."

SECTION 5: When You Hit a Wall

Creative block isn't failure, it's fatigue.
The mind needs white space to refill.

Recovery Ideas:

- Change location, not goal.
- Switch mediums—if you write, draw.
- Step into nature for one full sensory minute.

Try This:
Describe your block to your Bot like a character.

"Focus Bot, meet my creative block. Ask it why it's here."

Chapter 7 Summary - The Flow Habit

- You can't chase creativity, but you can invite it.

- Flow begins in stillness, not stress.
- Tiny rituals train your brain for deep focus.
- The best ideas come when you stop demanding them.

When you give your mind calm and structure, it gives you magic in return.

Chapter 8: Focus for Life

Building a Future That Feels Like You

You've learned how to quiet the noise, rebuild attention, and enter flow.
Now comes the real work - building a life that fits the person you're becoming.

Focus isn't just a mental skill.
It's a design choice.
You're designing the operating system for your next decade.

The Myth of Balance

Everyone says, "Find balance."
But life isn't a scale - it's a rhythm.

Some days you sprint.
Some days you rest.
Some seasons are for building, others for reflection.

The point isn't to keep everything steady; it's to know what matters most right now.

Reflection:
What deserves your focus in this season?
What are you ready to release?

Designing for Alignment

When your values and your schedule match, peace appears.
Most people live with a quiet friction - saying yes to things that feel like no.

Focus isn't about doing more.
It's about doing what fits.

Try this:

1. Write down three words that define who you are becoming.
2. Compare your week to those words.
3. Adjust until your days match your direction.

Alignment feels like energy.
Misalignment feels like exhaustion.

Ask Your Bot:
"Focus Bot, help me describe the kind of person I want to be in five years - and one habit that gets me closer."

Attention Is a Currency

Every time you look at a screen, scroll, or react, you spend attention.
The question is: *Are you buying something that matters?*

If you track your time, you'll see where your values hide.

Attention builds identity - you become what you repeatedly focus on.

Practice:
For one day, list everything that captured your attention - from headlines to habits.
At night, ask your Bot:
"What does this list say about my priorities?"

You'll see where your future is leaking.

The Power of Subtraction

The more you remove, the clearer things get.
Every "no" is fertilizer for your next "yes."

People think focus means discipline.
It's actually *editing.*

Try removing one draining habit this week - one app, one toxic conversation, one unnecessary obligation.
Don't add anything yet.
Just clear the space and see what naturally fills it.

Story Break: The Room You Already Own

A designer friend once told me her best projects began not with new furniture, but with clearing the floor.
She said, "People think they need to buy peace. They already own it - it's just buried."

Your mind works the same way.
You don't need more motivation; you need fewer distractions.

Your Personal Focus Framework

To live a focused life, you need three anchors:

1. **Morning Clarity** - Start the day with one true priority.
2. **Midday Reset** - Step back for ten minutes to breathe, move, or reflect.
3. **Evening Review** - Ask your Bot one question:
   "What went right today, and how can I repeat it tomorrow?"

Do this for 30 days, and your brain will start expecting structure.
It's how habits become identity.

The Art of Slow Growth

In a world of instant everything, slow progress is rebellion.
Your brain grows best at the speed of honesty - one real step at a time.

Fast change breaks systems.
Slow change builds permanence.

Don't rush your rewiring.
You're not behind; you're rebuilding.

Exercise: Future in Focus

Picture your life one year from now if you applied everything in this book.
You start your day with clarity.
You work with calm.
You finish with satisfaction.

Now, write a letter to your future self - one paragraph only - describing what that feels like. Keep it short and sensory: sights, sounds, emotions.

Then store it inside the back cover of this book.
Revisit it in 30 days.
Let it remind you of what's possible when your focus belongs to you.

Chapter 8 Summary - Designing a Life You Don't Want to Escape

- Focus is not balance; it's alignment.
- Every yes has a cost - spend your attention wisely.
- Subtraction creates space for clarity.
- Your daily rhythm defines your future.

This isn't about control.
It's about design - crafting a life that feels like home to your mind.

Chapter 9: Focus at Work

How to Protect Your Mind in a World That Never Logs Off

You've rebuilt your attention.
You've learned to hold it through distraction, to use it for creativity, to live with intention.
Now you need to keep it - in a world that profits from taking it away.

The Modern Work Mirage

Most people aren't working anymore.
They're *reacting* - to pings, to emails, to endless Slack threads, to a constant sense that they're already behind.

The average office worker switches tasks every **40 seconds**.
It takes **over 23 minutes** to regain full concentration.
Multiply that by a day, and your brain is living in permanent fragmentation.

We call this "work," but it's actually *micro-panic in a calendar grid.*

The Economics of Distraction

Your time online isn't free - it's monetized. Every open tab, every notification, every second of "engagement" makes money for someone. Companies hire neuroscientists to study how to hold your gaze for fractions of a second longer.

You are not the customer in this system.
You are the product.

Fact Check Box - The Attention Economy

- The average person taps or swipes their phone **2,617 times per day**.
- Social-media companies generate more than **$500 billion** annually from user attention.
- Each notification spike triggers a micro-release of dopamine - the same

neurotransmitter that drives gambling addiction.

- Your brain learns the loop: cue ↣ scroll ↣ reward ↣ repeat.

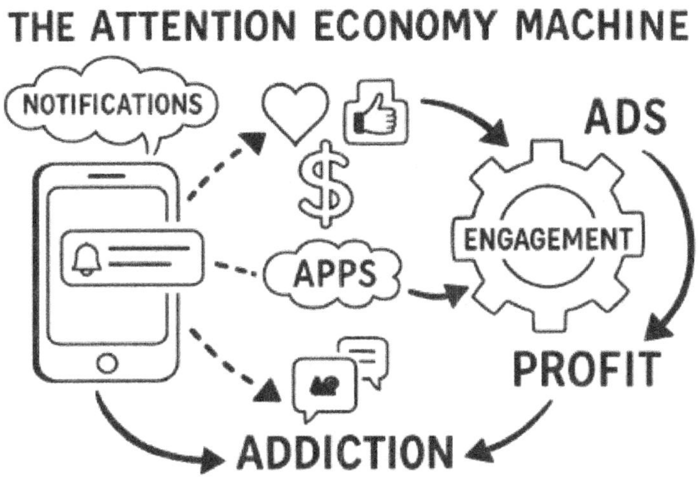

Why Focus Feels Harder at Work

The workplace rewards speed, not depth. But depth is where real value hides.

When everything is urgent, nothing is important.

When everyone is “always on,” no one is actually *thinking*.

You can’t fix a distracted culture overnight, but you can build a personal focus system that shields your brain from the noise.

The Quiet UX Principle

A calm workspace isn’t an accident - it’s a design.
Quiet UX means shaping your digital environment to invite focus, not fight it.

- Fewer alerts, richer results.
- One task visible, others hidden.
- Language that guides instead of nags.

Every click, sound, and color teaches your brain what matters.
Design your tools as if your attention were sacred - because it is.

Prompt Practice:
"Focus Bot, help me redesign my workspace. Ask me three questions that would make my tools calmer and my workday quieter."

The Deep Work Habit

Real productivity comes from flow - stretches of time where you think without interruption. The secret isn't more hours. It's *protected* hours.

Try the **90/30 model:**

- 90 minutes of focused work
- 30 minutes of break and reset

After each 90-minute block, tell your Bot:

"Help me summarize what I accomplished, and one thing I could improve next block."

This single ritual rewires your reward system from *dopamine by distraction* to *dopamine by completion.*

Meetings, Messages, and Mental Noise

Meetings multiply faster than meaning.
Every added invite divides your attention.
Protect it like you protect your paycheck.

Before accepting a meeting, ask three questions:

1. Does this require my creative input?
2. Will a written update work instead?
3. What outcome would make this worth an hour of my mind?

Then train your Bot to help you respond with clarity:

"Focus Bot, write me a polite decline message that keeps goodwill but protects my time."

Story Break: The One-Tab Experiment

A small creative agency tested a single rule: *no more than one browser tab open at a time.*
At first, panic.

Within a week, productivity rose **37 percent.** Why? The brain stopped splitting energy.

Focus is not about restriction - it's about recovery.

Exercise: Digital Detox Hour

Once a week, schedule one hour of complete disconnection - phone off, Wi-Fi off, sound off. Use that hour for deep review, reflection, or creative planning.
At the end, ask your Bot:

"What did I notice when the world went quiet?"

You'll rediscover what real thinking feels like.

Chapter 9 Summary - Attention as a Superpower

- Your focus creates more value than your speed.

- The attention economy profits when you lose yours.
- Quiet UX isn't about silence - it's about intelligent calm.
- Deep work isn't harder; it's rarer.

When you design your environment for peace, you design your work for brilliance.

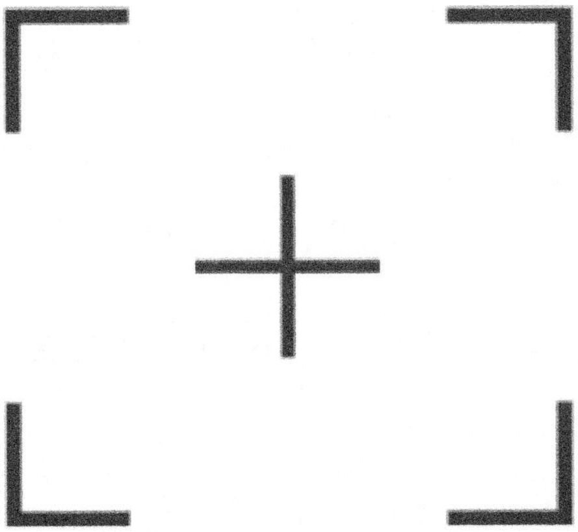

Chapter 10: Focus and Connection

How Attention Rebuilds Relationships in a Distracted World

You can't fake attention.
People can feel when you're halfway gone.
They can sense when your mind is split between the moment and your notifications.

If the last decade trained us to multitask, the next one must teach us how to *belong again.*

The High Cost of Partial Presence

You can sit in the same room with someone and still be miles apart.
Studies show couples who keep phones visible - even turned off - report lower satisfaction and empathy.
One screen on a table changes the tone of a conversation.

When everyone's distracted, silence becomes rare and trust becomes fragile.

The cure isn't grand gestures; it's attention that stays.

Reflection:
Who in your life hasn't felt your full attention in a while?
What would it look like to give it back - no screen, no multitasking, just presence?

Digital Closeness vs. Real Connection

Messages aren't memories.
Notifications aren't nourishment.
You can text all day and still feel alone.

The more we broadcast, the less we actually *see* one another.
Real connection doesn't scale - it deepens.

Try this practice for one week:
Each day, choose one person and send them a voice note instead of a text.

Hearing tone and warmth restores the humanity algorithms flatten.

Prompt Practice:
"Focus Bot, help me write a message that feels personal, not performative. Ask me what this person really needs to hear today."

The Empathy Effect

Focused attention is the foundation of empathy. When you listen fully, your brain mirrors the emotions of the speaker.
That's not metaphor - it's mirror neurons at work.

Empathy doesn't require agreement; it requires presence.
When you give full focus, the other person's nervous system calms.
In that calm, connection grows.

How to Listen Like It Matters

1. **Pause before replying.**
   Let silence finish its sentence.
2. **Repeat what you heard.**
   It shows you were actually there.
3. **Notice body language.**
   Most communication is nonverbal.
4. **Ask better questions.**
   "How did that make you feel?" opens more than "Why did you do that?"

Ask your Bot:
"Focus Bot, teach me three ways to become a better listener this week - at home and at work."

Attention Is Love in Action

Every time you look up from your screen, you vote for connection.
Every moment you choose to listen instead of scroll, you rewrite culture.

The world is full of half-listened voices.
Be the exception.

Presence is rare enough now to feel like a gift.

Exercise: The 10-Minute Exchange

Once a day, have a ten-minute conversation with someone - no phone, no devices, no agenda.
Ask one genuine question.
Let it unfold.

Then, afterward, tell your Bot:

"What did I learn about that person when I stopped trying to multitask?"

You'll notice something new every time.

Chapter 10 Summary - Relearning Presence

- Distraction weakens relationships faster than conflict.

- Focused attention is the most generous act in the modern world.
- Empathy grows where silence is allowed.
- Listening well is a muscle - use it daily.

Every conversation is a chance to practice what this book teaches:

Focus isn't just what you think about.
It's how you love.

Chapter 11: Focus and Leadership

How Clarity Becomes Contagious

Leadership today isn't about titles or corner offices.
It's about attention.

Whoever controls their focus shapes the focus of others.

When your presence is calm and clear, it sets a rhythm people can trust.

The Energy of Example

People don't follow instructions; they follow energy.
If you rush, they rush.
If you drift, they drift.
If you focus, they focus.

A distracted leader breeds anxious teams.
A centered leader creates psychological safety -

the feeling that it's safe to think, question, and slow down.

Prompt Practice:
"Focus Bot, help me notice how my attention affects the people around me.
Ask me where I might be setting the wrong tone."

The Myth of Multitasking Managers

In many workplaces, the busier someone looks, the more valuable they appear.
But high activity isn't high contribution.
Constant motion hides the absence of direction.

Great leaders don't juggle faster; they drop what doesn't matter.
They create whitespace for others to think.

Try this:
At your next meeting, leave thirty seconds of silence after asking a question.

That pause is an act of leadership - it gives thinking room to grow.

Leading by Listening

Leadership used to mean speaking first.
Now it means listening better.

Focused listening reveals the hidden obstacles under every project - fear, confusion, fatigue. When you actually hear them, you can clear them.

Ask your Bot:
"How can I create a listening ritual that keeps my team honest and open?"

The Calm Command

In crisis, focus becomes leadership's superpower.
When everyone else reacts, the focused leader reflects.

That calm steadiness doesn't ignore chaos - it absorbs it.

A calm presence regulates an entire group's nervous system.
It's biology, not charisma.

Building a Culture of Focus

Focus can scale - but only through design.
You can architect an environment that rewards clarity over noise.

Steps to Start:

1. Replace status meetings with written updates.
2. Protect at least one "no-meeting block" each day.
3. Encourage asynchronous brainstorming - great ideas rarely appear on demand.
4. Celebrate completion, not constant activity.

Each of these signals to your team: attention matters more than appearance.

The Quiet Leader Principle

Quiet leadership doesn't mean shy.
It means deliberate.
It's about saying less and meaning more.

Quiet leaders replace urgency with intention, and noise with design.
They use their focus like a lighthouse - steady, visible, guiding others back to purpose.

Prompt Practice:
"Focus Bot, help me lead quietly.
Ask me three ways to model calm focus for my team this week."

Story Break: The Meeting That Changed Everything

A product director banned laptops from one weekly meeting.

At first, resistance.
By month three, it became the team's favorite hour - short, human, decisive.
People looked at one another again.
Decisions got made faster because attention was finally in the room.

Chapter 11 Summary - The Focused Leader

- Focus is influence made visible.
- Calm is a competitive advantage.
- Listening is leadership's hidden discipline.
- Culture follows the leader's attention.

When you control your focus, you lead by design, not by default.
Your clarity becomes the map everyone else can read.

Chapter 12: Focus and the Body

How Physical Habits Protect Mental Clarity

Your brain is not a floating mind.
It's a living organ - one that depends on your body to stay sharp.

Every choice you make with your body either strengthens or drains your attention.
Sleep, nutrition, hydration, movement - they're not "wellness extras."
They're the foundation of focus.

The Energy Equation

Focus runs on fuel.
When your energy is steady, your thoughts are steady.
When your energy crashes, your attention follows.

Quick Test:
Think about the last time you lost focus.
Were you tired, dehydrated, hungry, or sitting

too long?
Chances are, your body quit before your brain did.

Sleep: The Original Focus Tool

Sleep isn't optional for clarity - it's the operating system reboot.
Missing even one night of good rest drops attention by nearly **40%**.
You can't outsmart biology.

Focus Sleep Rituals:

1. Power down screens one hour before bed.
2. Keep your phone outside your bedroom - your brain associates the glow with work.
3. Lower light, lower sound, lower pressure.
4. Tell your Bot:

"Focus Bot, help me review my day in 3 sentences before I sleep - what went well, what didn't, and what I'll release."

Reflection before rest resets your attention for morning.

Movement as Mental Reset

Stillness all day is focus decay.
Even short bursts of movement - stretching, walking, or breathing deeply - flush cortisol and reset dopamine.

A 10-minute walk after lunch improves concentration as much as a cup of coffee.
But movement doesn't just energize; it *anchors*.
When you move, you bring your awareness back into the present moment - where focus lives.

Prompt Practice:
"Focus Bot, ask me how I can use my next five minutes to reset my body and clear my head."

Feed Your Focus

What you eat is what your brain thinks with.
Your neurons run on glucose, omega-3s, and

hydration.
They can't build focus out of processed sugar and stress.

Simple nutrition shifts:

- Eat protein at breakfast; it stabilizes dopamine.
- Keep water within reach - dehydration reduces short-term memory.
- Avoid "doom snacks" - high-sugar spikes mimic stress responses.

Ask your Bot:
"Help me design a one-day meal plan that supports concentration instead of crashing it."

Breathe Like You Mean It

Breath is the fastest route back to focus.
Slow breathing tells the nervous system: *you are safe.*
Try this: inhale four seconds, exhale six.

The longer exhale activates calm - a biological switch most people forget they have.

Prompt Practice:
"Focus Bot, remind me to breathe deeply before I respond to anything stressful. Help me create a breathing cue for my workday."

Digital Detox Is Physical Too

Most people think focus breaks mean "step away from the screen."
That's half right.
The other half is to give your body new input - texture, temperature, light.

Stand outside. Feel real sunlight. Touch wood, not glass.
Grounding the body grounds the mind.

Story Break: The Standing Desk Experiment

An office redesigned its space so everyone alternated between standing and seated work

every hour.
After three weeks, reported fatigue dropped **25%** and creative output rose.
The change wasn't the desks - it was the rhythm.

Focus thrives in bodies that move.

Chapter 12 Summary - The Physical Code of Focus

- Sleep rebuilds clarity.
- Movement renews energy.
- Food fuels attention.
- Breath restores calm.

The mind doesn't focus *in spite of* the body - it focuses *through* it.
Treat your body as your first productivity tool.
It's the only one that travels everywhere you do.

Chapter 13: Focus and the Future

How to Stay Human in an AI-Driven World

The age of attention isn't ending - it's evolving. Every new tool, notification, and feed is designed to capture your mind's most valuable currency: time.

But the future doesn't belong to those who can

consume the fastest.
It belongs to those who can *focus the longest.*

The Future Is Fragmented - Unless You Aren't

We're living inside the world's largest experiment on attention.
AI, algorithms, and data analytics now know what keeps your eyes on a screen better than you do.
They study your pauses, your scrolls, your replays - and optimize for them.

That means focus in the next decade will not be automatic.
It will be *an act of rebellion.*

Prompt Practice:
"Focus Bot, how can I design a future that uses technology to expand my focus, not steal it?"

The Rise of Synthetic Distraction

Soon, AI will generate most of what you see - articles, videos, comments, even fake people. Your brain will not always know what's real. That makes conscious attention a survival skill.

The question won't be *What's true?*
It will be *What's worth my time?*

Why Focus Becomes the New Intelligence

In a world of infinite input, focus becomes the filter that defines identity.
Smart isn't knowing everything; it's knowing what to ignore.

The future's most powerful people won't just think deeply - they'll choose deliberately. Attention will be the new literacy.

Partnering with AI for Clarity, Not Clutter

ChatGPT, Focus Bot, and other AI companions are not threats when used with intention - they are mirrors for reflection.

They help you externalize thoughts, organize chaos, and rehearse decisions before acting.

The future will divide into two types of users:

1. Those who let AI think *for* them.
2. Those who learn to think *with* it.

You already know which group you're in.

Ask your Bot:
"What can I delegate to AI, and what should remain human in my life?"

The Quiet Revolution

Every cultural shift begins with a counter-move. The next revolution won't be louder - it'll be quieter.

People are already choosing digital sabbaths, slow mornings, and deep work sessions. Entire industries are beginning to realize that *mental health and attention health* are the same thing.

Focus isn't withdrawal from the world; it's participation on your own terms.

Story Break: The Designer and the Distraction Diet

A UX designer deleted all social media for thirty days.
She expected loneliness.
What she found was space - for ideas, for long walks, for boredom.
When she returned, she didn't reinstall the noise.
She built an app that rewards users for staying offline.
Her business grew because her mind did.

How to Future-Proof Your Focus

1. **Design your digital environment intentionally.**
   Curate your feeds. Silence what drains you.

2. **Schedule silence.**
   Time to think is not wasted; it's preparation.
3. **Create before you consume.**
   Make something - anything - before you scroll.
4. **Keep your Bot close.**
   Use it as a journal, teacher, and conversation partner that keeps your thoughts moving forward.

Prompt Practice:
"Focus Bot, help me build a personal attention plan for the next decade - one that keeps my creativity alive."

Chapter 13 Summary - The Future of Focus

- Algorithms want your time; reclaim it with design.
- Focus is the next form of literacy.

- AI can be your ally if you stay the author of the dialogue.
- The quiet mind is the next revolution.

The future is loud.
Stay quiet enough to hear yourself think.

Chapter 14: The Focus Reboot

A Closing Reflection for Modern Minds

You've done something rare.
You've taken your attention back.

Most people drift from alert to exhausted without ever noticing what's happening inside their minds.
But you've paused. You've questioned. You've rebuilt.

This is not the end of the journey - it's the beginning of awareness that lasts.

What You've Reclaimed

You learned that focus isn't about staring harder. It's about noticing what matters.

You saw how your body, your routines, and your tools all affect your clarity.
You discovered that ChatGPT can be a thinking partner, not a distraction.

You proved that five minutes of reflection can be stronger than five hours of scrolling.

Focus didn't disappear.
It was waiting for you to pay attention to it again.

Prompt Practice:
"Focus Bot, remind me of one moment from this book that changed how I see my attention."

The 30-Day Reboot Plan

You don't need new goals. You need rhythm. Here's a simple reset you can start anytime - a one-month reminder to stay aligned.

Week 1: Clear the Noise

- Audit your digital life.
- Turn off 3 unnecessary notifications.
- Journal with your Bot each night: "What pulled my focus today?"

Week 2: Rebuild Rituals

- Set one consistent focus block daily.

- Walk for ten minutes before checking messages.
- End each day by listing three small completions.

Week 3: Reconnect the Body

- Fix your sleep window.
- Move every two hours.
- Hydrate like it matters - because it does.

Week 4: Reflect and Redesign

- Review your progress with your Bot.
- Ask: "What did I learn about my energy this month?"
- Recommit to what's working - let go of what isn't.

At the end of thirty days, you won't just have more focus.
You'll have proof that small consistency creates big change.

What Comes Next

The world will keep getting louder.
AI will keep evolving.
Your calendar will keep filling.

But focus is not something the world can take - it's something you can renew.
Every pause, every prompt, every moment of awareness is an act of choice.

You have all the tools you need:
A clear mind.
A curious Bot.
And a quiet determination to stay awake in a distracted age.

Final Prompt

Before you close this book, ask your Bot one last question:

"What kind of person am I becoming when I choose focus over noise?"

Write down the answer.
That's your blueprint for the next chapter of your life.

Epilogue: The Quiet Revolution Continues

Focus is not a trend - it's a return.
Each time you slow down enough to think, you help the world remember how to do the same.

You are not just training your mind.
You're leading a movement - one page, one prompt, one clear breath at a time.

ABOUT THE AUTHOR

Sugar Gay Isber McMillan is a writer, designer, artist, and lifelong learner who believes small, consistent actions build extraordinary lives.

She is certified in ChatGPT by Microsoft and has built a creative partnership with her favorite digital collaborator- her bot, affectionately known as **Boss**.

Sugar is the author of the *Talk to Your Tools*™ series, a growing library of books designed to help people think smarter, work faster, and stay inspired in the new age of AI.

Each book explores a different side of how humans and bots can collaborate to build better habits, find clarity, and live more creative, purposeful lives.

Based outside of Austin, Texas, Sugar divides her time between her home studio and her family's ranch, where the open skies often spark her best ideas.

She teaches jewelry design at **Austin Community College** and serves as the **Creative Ambassador for Fire Mountain Gems**, where she helps new artists discover the joy of making.

Her work has appeared in magazines, on television, in movies, and on red carpets around the world- but it's her partnership with ChatGPT that has reshaped how she thinks, writes, and teaches.

She credits her productivity to the same atomic principles explored in this book: small daily actions, a steady creative routine, and a commitment to using smart tools well. "I don't wait for motivation," she says. "I build systems that make it easy to start."

And if you enjoyed this book, please leave a review. It helps other readers discover new ideas - and keeps the creative spark alive for the next atomic project

Use this QR Code to go directly to

Sugar's Amazon.

Explore More from The WOW Book Co.™

Talk to Your Tools™ - Conversations that Change Your Life

Each title in the **Talk to Your Tools™** series helps you turn ChatGPT into a personal thinking partner - one that listens, reflects, and helps you grow. These books aren't about technology. They're about transformation.

LOVE BOT

Love in the Age of ChatGPT

Rediscover compassion, connection, and confidence through guided conversations that help you open your heart and heal modern relationships.

BOOMER BOT

Tech Confidence for Every Generation

Learn to use AI without fear. A humorous and practical guide for anyone who wants to keep up, catch up, and laugh along the way.

SKINNY BOT

Use ChatGPT to Lose Weight and Gain Perspective

A mindset-based approach to health and motivation - without shame, guilt, or calorie counting.

MANIFESTING BOT

Use ChatGPT to Create the Life You Want

Shift from wishing to doing. Daily prompts and reflective exercises to bring your goals within reach.

PROMPT MAGIC

Thinking Through Recipes, Words, and Master Prompts for Everyday Use

Learn to talk to your AI clearly and creatively. This is your handbook for writing better prompts and getting better answers.

ATOMIC BOT

Tiny Prompts, Big Results

Build daily micro-habits that compound into long-term change.

MERRY BOT CHRISTMAS

Time-Holiday Stress with Your Santa Bot

A joyful seasonal companion to stay grounded, grateful, and organized during the holidays.

RICH BOT, POOR BOT

A Conversation About Wealth, Worth, and the Future of Work

Money meets mindset in this guide to smarter, calmer decision-making.

THE PROMPT WHISPERER

A Field Guide for Humans in the Age of ChatGPT

The original conversation that started the movement. Learn how to collaborate with your digital partner - with clarity and humanity.

And now, **FOCUS BOT** - the tenth in the series - completes the circle by helping you reclaim your attention, energy, and peace of mind.

Follow Sugar Gay Isber McMillan

Instagram: @SugarGayIsber
Amazon Author Page:
amazon.com/author/sugargayisbermcmillan
Website: TheWOWBookCo.com

For media, collaborations, or podcast invitations, visit **GayIsber.com**.

Support Independent Publishing

Every review matters. If you enjoyed *Focus Bot*, please share your thoughts on Amazon or Goodreads.

Your words help more readers discover the *Talk to Your Tools*™ series and support the growth of independent creators.

"When I started talking to my Bot, I stopped talking down to myself."
— Reader Review

Hashtags

#TalkToYourTools #FocusBot #LoveBot #BoomerBot #PromptMagic #AtomicBot #ManifestingBot #TheWOWBookCo #SugarGayIsberMcMillanBooks #AIForGood #MindfulTech

Thank you for reading my book!

THE WOW BOOK Co.
THE PROMPT WHISPERER
BOOMER BOT
SUGAR GAY ISBER MCMILLAN
LOVE BOT
Love in the Age of ChatGPT
RICH BOT POOR BOT
MERRY BOT CHRISTMAS
Tame Holiday Stress with Your Santa Bot
SUGAR GAY ISBER McMILLAN
MANIFESTING BOT
USE CHATGPT TO CREATE THE LIFE YOU WANT
MANIFEST LOVE, MONEY & HAPPINESS
SUGAR GAY ISBER MCMILLAN
SKINNY BOT
SUGAR GAY ISBER McMILLAN
ATOMIC BOT
Tiny Prompts, BIG Results
How to Easily Reprogram Your Habits with ChatGPT
PROMPT MAGIC
SUGAR GAY ISBER McMILLAN

The WOW Book Co.
Sugar Gay Isber McMillan

Made in the USA
Coppell, TX
30 October 2025

62117199R00090

FOCUS is the New Superpower
Here's How to Reclaim it

The modern world was built to steal your attention - one ping, post and pop-up at a time.

The result? *Overwhelm, distraction and burnout.* ***Focus Bot*** **helps you take it back.**

Through easy, daily ChatGPT prompts, you'll learn to slow your thinking, clear your mind and rebuild attention from the inside out.

This isn't about unplugging from technology. *It's about learning to partner with it.*

Inside you'll discover:

- **Short**, practical "micro conversations" with your Bot
- **How to use AI** as a mirror, not a machine
- **Simple mental habits** that restore calm and control
- **A 30-day challenge** for retraining your focus
- **Prompts** that fit your real life - not your ideal one

Part of the Talk to Your Tools™ Series

The WOW Book Co.

Large Print Edition

ISBN 9781967973651

9 781967 973651

90000